THE BRIDGE
and Other Love Stories

Love can always find a way, people say. But the road to love is often difficult. People say the wrong thing, do the wrong thing, can't find the right words, make mistakes, misunderstand each other . . .

In the first story Luke and Gemma talk about a plan for love. But who makes the plan? And who is the plan for? What kind of plan? You can make a plan for a holiday or a train journey or a piece of work, but can you really make a plan for love?

In the second story Sam plans a big surprise at the Sunflower Café for his girlfriend Lucy. Sam makes wonderful cakes, and the surprise is a nice idea. But what does Lucy think about it?

In the last story Alma returns to her home town after six years away. It is a sad time for her, because she cannot forget the story of Nina and Dragan. Nina was Alma's sister, and Nina was in love with a young man called Dragan . . .

OXFORD BOOKWORMS LIBRARY

Human Interest

The Bridge
and Other Love Stories

Stage 1 (400 headwords)

Series Editor: Jennifer Bassett
Founder Editor: Tricia Hedge
Activities Editors: Jennifer Bassett and Christine Lindop

AUTHOR'S NOTE

The story *The Bridge* was inspired by the report of the deaths of Bosko Brckic and Admira Ismic in Sarajevo in 1993. Some people called them the Romeo and Juliet of Sarajevo. But this is not their story. My story *The Bridge* takes the same idea of young lovers in a city at war, and makes a new story – of sadness and death, but of love and hope too.

Christine Lindop

CHRISTINE LINDOP

The Bridge

and Other Love Stories

Illustrated by
Jérôme Mireault

OXFORD UNIVERSITY PRESS

OXFORD
UNIVERSITY PRESS

Great Clarendon Street, Oxford, OX2 6DP, United Kingdom

Oxford University Press is a department of the University of Oxford.
It furthers the University's objective of excellence in research, scholarship,
and education by publishing worldwide. Oxford is a registered trade
mark of Oxford University Press in the UK and in certain other countries

ISBN: 978 0 19 479368 1

A complete recording of this Bookworms edition of
The Bridge and Other Love Stories is available on audio CD. ISBN: 0 19 479366 7

Printed in China

Word count (main text): 5,605 words

For more information on the Oxford Bookworms Library,
visit www.oup.com/elt/bookworms

ACKNOWLEDGEMENTS
Illustrations by: Jérôme Mireault, colagene.com

CONTENTS

Plan for Love

♡   ೪

Gemma was hungry. Time for lunch, she thought. She went down to the hospital canteen, got some sandwiches and a cup of coffee, and looked for a table. But it was one o'clock and the canteen was very busy. There were no free tables. Then, at the long table by the window, she saw a tall man with fair hair. It was her friend Luke, and there was a seat next to him. She walked across to him.

'Hi Luke. Can I sit here?' said Gemma.

Luke did not look up, and did not speak. Perhaps he didn't hear her.

Gemma tried again. 'Luke? Er, can I sit here? Or are you waiting for someone?'

'Oh, hi Gemma. No, no, I'm not waiting for anyone. Come and sit down.'

Gemma put her sandwiches and coffee on the table, and sat down. She and Luke worked in the physiotherapy clinic in a hospital in Bristol. Usually, Luke was friendly, but not today.

'The canteen's very busy,' Gemma said. 'Where did all these people come from?'

Luke did not answer.

'Luke? Are you OK? Is something wrong?'

'I'm OK. I'm good,' said Luke. He moved his coffee cup around on the table, and did not look at Gemma. He drank some coffee. Gemma began to eat her sandwiches.

Then Luke put his cup down, and looked at Gemma. 'Gemma, we're good friends, aren't we? Can I talk to you?'

Gemma put her sandwich down. 'Yes, of course, Luke. What is it?'

Luke's face was red. 'It's stupid of me, I know that. But I . . . I mean . . . Look, do you see that girl over there? The girl with the long blonde hair?'

Gemma looked across the canteen. There was a beautiful girl with long blonde hair at a table near the door. Gemma's hair was short and black, and she wore glasses.

'You mean Charlotte? She works for Dr Howell, doesn't she?'

'That's right. Well, I really like her. She's . . . well, look at her, she's beautiful! I want to talk to her, I really do!'

'So talk to her!'

'But I can never find the right words. What can I say? I open my mouth – and nothing comes out! And she goes away, and I feel stupid.'

Gemma smiled at him.

'Poor Luke! But that's not like you. When you're with me, you talk about lots of things. Like this weekend – what did you do this weekend?'

'I went swimming with Paul on Saturday,' Luke said.
'We went in the sea. It was so cold – but it was great!'
  They talked for a few minutes. Then Gemma said:
'Luke, you're on the social committee, aren't you?'

'Do you see that girl over there?' said Luke.

'Yes, that's right,' said Luke. 'Why?'

'Well, I've got a plan. We make you a list of questions – about music, and free time, nights out – things like that. Then you ask Charlotte these questions. You're asking them for the social committee, you see. And she answers – and you ask some more questions, and there you are . . . you're talking to Charlotte!'

'Hmm,' said Luke. 'Yes, I see – I think!'

'I know,' said Gemma, 'let's try the plan now. You're Charlotte, and I'm Luke. I do the questions, and you do the answers – OK?'

'Er, yes,' said Luke. 'You mean, I must ask you all these questions now?'

'Er, no,' said Gemma. 'It's like . . . well, we're playing . . . I'm playing Luke, and you're playing Charlotte. For now, you ARE Charlotte, OK?'

'Right. Got it,' said Luke. 'So you're me. You're Luke.'

Gemma smiled again. 'Good. OK, let's go.' She spoke in a different voice. 'Hi Charlotte. My name's Luke, and I'm on the social committee. We want to plan some days and nights out for people from the hospital. What do *you* like doing? Is it OK to ask you some questions?'

'Yes, of course,' said Luke.

'OK – first, what kind of music do you like?'

'That's easy. I like Black Phoenix, and the Tree Rats – do you know the Tree Rats? They're really good.'

'No, I don't,' said Gemma, 'but I saw Black Phoenix

'You just need the questions,' said Gemma.

last month. They're great! OK – what do you like doing at the weekend?'

'I like running, and swimming,' said Luke. 'And I like going out on my bike . . .'

'You see?' said Gemma. 'It's easy really. You just need the questions.'

♡
⸻
ஃ

Later that afternoon, Luke stopped in the office. Gemma was at one of the computers.

'Hi, Luke,' said Gemma. 'Have you got a few minutes? I've got some questions here. Come and see.'

Luke read the list of questions on her computer.

'Oh, that's great, Gemma!' he said.

'Do you want to put any more questions on the list?' she asked. Luke thought for a minute.

'Do you like going to music festivals?' he said at last.

'Yes, that's good,' said Gemma. She put it on the list. Soon Luke had the list in his hands.

'Wait for the right time,' said Gemma. 'And – good luck!'

♡
⚥

Every day Luke looked for Charlotte in the canteen. On Tuesday she was with Molly, and on Wednesday he did not see her. But on Thursday . . .

'Hi Charlotte,' said Luke. 'My name's Luke. I'm on the social committee. We want to plan some days and nights out for people from the hospital. Can I ask you some questions?'

'OK,' said Charlotte, and she smiled at Luke.

They sat down near the window.

'Right,' said Luke. 'First, what kind of music do you like?'

'Well, I like the Good Girls, and Sadie Moonlight, and lots of girl singers, really. Oh, and Bobbie, of course.'

'Bobbie?' said Luke. 'Really?'

'He's *wonderful*. "Love me, love nobody but me,"' sang Charlotte happily.

'Do you like Black Phoenix?'

'Who?' said Charlotte.

'Um – it doesn't matter,' said Luke quickly. 'Let's see – do you like swimming?'

'Swimming?' laughed Charlotte. 'Just look at my hair. Me – swimming!'

'Have you got a bike?'

'No – I rode a bike when I was little, but not now. Not in these shoes.' Luke looked at Charlotte's shoes. They had very high heels.

'Swimming?' laughed Charlotte. 'Just look at my hair!'

'Do you go to festivals?'

'Only in good weather, with no rain and no tents.'

'So – you never go to festivals,' Luke said.

'Never,' said Charlotte.

'What *do* you like doing in your free time then?'

'Facebook,' Charlotte said. 'I'm on Facebook every night. Are you on Facebook?'

'Er, no,' said Luke. 'I, er, use computers at work, but away from work I like to do other things. I go—'

But Charlotte was not interested in listening to Luke. 'But why not?' she said. 'Facebook is soooo cool! Do you know, I've got 778 Facebook friends, lots of them are in America, and I've got some in Japan, Australia – oh, everywhere! And photos – I've got thousands of photos on Facebook now.'

'You don't go out much, then?' Luke asked. 'You just go on Facebook?'

'Of course not!' said Charlotte. 'Don't be stupid. I hang out with my friends – Monica, Jess, Ellie, Alice . . . We go to clubs, and we go shopping. I *love* shopping. We're going to Eastwater next weekend, me and Jess and Alice. Do you know, there are more than 250 shops there. We're going into every one of them! I can't wait!' She saw Luke's face, and laughed. 'Oh, men are soooo boring about shopping!'

'Well, I, er . . .' Luke said. He began again. '250 shops – Wow! That's a lot of shopping. Well, have a great day

'I love shopping. We're going to Eastwater next weekend . . .'

with your friends, Charlotte. Thanks for your time. Nice talking to you.'

'That's OK, Luke,' said Charlotte. 'Bye.'

Gemma looked up. Luke was at the door, and in his hand was the list of questions.

'Hmm,' she said. 'That's not a happy face. Three out of ten? Two out of ten?'

'Zero out of ten, I think,' said Luke unhappily. 'She

doesn't like swimming, bikes, or festivals, and she doesn't like Black Phoenix – she likes Bobbie!'

'Bobbie!' said Gemma. She laughed. 'Oh no!'

'Yes. And she likes the Good Girls. And she loves shopping, and can't wait to go to Eastwater.'

'Bad luck, Luke,' said Gemma. 'You got all the answers, but they're all the wrong answers. You and Charlotte are *very* different people.'

'Very different,' said Luke unhappily. 'You're right.'

He walked away, and Gemma watched him. 'Oh, Luke!' she thought.

♡
♈

On Sunday morning Luke went out on his bike. He rode along the streets of the city and thought about his week.

'I'm stupid,' he thought. 'Charlotte is the wrong girl for me. She's beautiful, but we like different things.'

Suddenly he saw a lot of people by the road. He stopped to look. 'What's going on?' he thought. 'Why are all those people clapping and shouting?' He began to cross the street, but a policeman came over to him.

'You can't go along there,' he said. 'The race is finishing there.'

'The race?' said Luke. 'What race is that?'

'It's the City Road Race,' said the policeman. 'Look – here come the runners now.'

The first man finished the race, and Luke clapped. A few minutes later, the women runners arrived. Luke clapped them too. Then he looked again. Was that Gemma? Yes it was – and she was third!

'Gemma,' Luke called. 'Well done, Gemma!' He put his bike against a tree and ran across to Gemma.

'Hello, Luke,' said Gemma. She was in her running clothes, black and green, and she looked good.

Gemma was in her running clothes, and she looked good.

'Wow,' Luke said. 'You look great in those colours. I only ever see you in hospital clothes usually. And you came third too. That's wonderful!'

Gemma was busy with her towel. 'Thanks, Luke,' she said.

Luke could not take his eyes away from Gemma. 'You're a runner,' he said. 'I never knew that.'

'You never asked me,' said Gemma. She smiled at Luke, a long slow warm smile.

Luke looked down into her blue eyes. He looked for a long time. A new and wonderful idea came into his head. 'Wow,' he said again. 'I never saw your eyes before – they're . . . beautiful.'

Gemma laughed. 'I wear glasses at work,' she said. 'That's why.'

Luke suddenly remembered. 'Hey, you're tired, you just ran a race. Let's sit down.'

They sat down on a low wall together. Around them, other people talked about the race, but Luke and Gemma did not hear them or see them. They sat quietly and Gemma drank some water. Luke wanted to say a lot of things, but he could not find the right words. Then he opened his mouth – and all the right words came out.

'Gemma, have you got a bike?' he asked.

'Yes,' she said. 'Last year I went to Utrecht for a week in the summer, and I went everywhere by bike.'

'Do you like swimming?'

'Yes, and I love swimming in the sea – it's the best.'

'And you like Black Phoenix, and the Tree Rats.'

'And Darkwater,' said Gemma. 'They're like the Tree Rats, but better.'

'Darkwater?' said Luke. 'I like them, they're really great. Hey, they're at the Mountain Club tonight. Would you like to . . . I mean . . . Do you . . . You don't want to come with me, perhaps?'

Gemma laughed, a long happy laugh. 'Of course, I want to!' she said. 'What time shall we go?'

Two things, Luke thought. You only need two things. The right questions – and the right answers. Then it's easy.

The Maker of Cakes

∞ 🧁 ∞

Friday, 8th February, afternoon
There was a noise under Lucy's desk. It was her mobile phone, with a new text message.

> Am away this weekend.
> Wed 13th, salsa dancing
> at Marco's Club. U coming?
> From: B
> 14:30 8-FEB-10

Lucy smiled. The message was from B – her good friend Becky. Becky was always busy with something new – new clothes, a new club, a new man . . . She was a beautiful girl, and of course men liked her.

Lucy sent a text back.

> 13th OK.
> From: Lucy
> 14:35 8-FEB-10

Lucy's boyfriend Sam was always busy on the 13th February, because the 14th was Valentine's Day. Sam made cakes, and had a cake shop and café called the Sunflower Café. Everybody in the town loved Sam's wonderful Valentine cakes. On the 14th February every year, the window of the Sunflower Café was full of them. 'Be my valentine!' they said, or 'Love me always.'

Lucy looked out of the window. Love me always! Oh yes, she loved Sam. They met three Christmases ago at a party. Sam was tall and quiet, but he was full of good ideas. Soon he and Lucy went everywhere together.

Sam and Lucy met three Christmases ago at a party.

'Is it love?' asked Becky after the first year.

'Of course it is,' said Lucy.

'Well, does he say, "Lucy, I can't live without you! Lucy, marry me! Be my valentine, always." Does he say all those things?' laughed Becky.

Lucy laughed too. 'No, that's not Sam. Sam doesn't *say* things – he *does* things.'

But today, Lucy thought, 'Three years is a long time to love somebody. Perhaps this year . . . Perhaps this Valentine's Day . . . Perhaps.'

Monday, 11th February, afternoon

Becky phoned Lucy on the 11th. 'I saw Sam this morning,' she said. 'He's so nice, Lucy – you're a lucky girl.'

Lucy was surprised. 'Where did you see him, Becky?'

'At the Sunflower Café, of course. I went there for a coffee.'

'Again?' Lucy thought. 'She went there three times last week, twice the week before . . . The Sunflower isn't near her office. Why does she always go there for coffee?'

'Oh,' she said. 'Well, Sam's very busy just now. I'm not going to see him for a day or two.'

Becky laughed. 'We've got a surprise for you, you know,' she said. 'I'm so excited. Can you wait for a few days?'

'*We've* got a surprise? What do you mean?' asked Lucy.

'We've got a surprise for you,' Becky laughed.

'I can't say anything now,' Becky answered. 'See you on the 13th. Bye.'

Suddenly Lucy wasn't so excited about Valentine's Day. She began to feel worried about her Sam – and beautiful Becky. What surprise? She didn't want any surprises. And a surprise from Sam *and* Becky? Becky often went to have coffee at Sam's café these days. Why? And Sam liked Becky, he often said that. He laughed a lot when he was with Becky. Perhaps he was in love with Becky. He didn't phone last night, he didn't phone the night before . . .

Wednesday, 13th February, afternoon

Late on the 13th, the Sunflower Café was busy. There were beautiful cakes everywhere, and people went out of the shop with happy smiles on their faces and big red boxes in their hands.

Lucy looked in, and saw Becky and Sam, heads together.

Sam went outside and looked at the window. He had a plan for Valentine's Day, and he was nearly ready.

'Hello, Sam.' It was Becky.

'Hi, Becky. Are you meeting Lucy?'

'Yes, we're going salsa dancing tonight. So – what's going in the window, Sam?'

'Ah, I've got a new idea. It's your idea, but better! Come into the shop.'

A moment later Lucy arrived at the door of the shop. She wanted to see Sam before she went dancing with Becky. She looked in, and saw Becky – Becky and Sam, heads together, talking and laughing. Lucy stopped at the door. 'So it's true,' she thought. 'There they are, together.' She could not hear their words, but they looked happy, so happy. Then Becky suddenly kissed Sam on the cheek, and Sam kissed Becky back.

Lucy went quietly away, her eyes full of tears. 'My heart is breaking,' she thought. 'I love him so much – but lots of men like beautiful Becky, and now he does too.'

She took out her phone and sent a text to Becky.

> Sorry. Not feeling well.
> Going home to bed.
> From: Lucy
> 17:40   13-FEB-10

Sam put his cakes in the window, and smiled. Becky went dancing, and laughed. Lucy went to bed – and cried.

Thursday, 14th February, morning

Lucy woke up the next morning. 'It's Valentine's Day,' she thought happily – but then she remembered Sam and Becky, and the happy smile left her face. Did it really happen?

But it *was* Valentine's Day. She waited until nearly nine o'clock. Perhaps a letter, some flowers, a cake from Sam? But nothing came.

Becky phoned. 'Are you OK, Lucy? How are you feeling today? Do you want to meet me at lunchtime at the Sunflower?'

'I – I don't know,' Lucy said. But she did know. She didn't want to see Sam and Becky together. She needed some time. 'It's going to be busy at work today,' she said. 'Perhaps later, OK?'

Then a text message arrived from Sam.

> Can you meet me at the café?
> From: Sam
> 08:55   14-FEB-10

Lucy sent her answer.

> Perhaps later.
> From: Lucy
> 08:59   14-FEB-10

But I'm not going to see Sam, she said to herself, and I'm not going to see Becky – and I'm not going to the shop. Valentines, love, hearts, kisses – no, thank you. And she turned off her phone and went to work.

Thursday, 14th February, afternoon

Later that afternoon Lucy turned on her phone again.
There were two texts, one from Becky . . .

> Come to the café. Exciting news!
>
> From: B
>
> 16:32   14-FEB-10

and another from Sam . . .

> Come to the café. Exciting news!
>
> From: Sam
>
> 16:35   14-FEB-10

But Becky sent her text at 16.32, and Sam sent his text
just three minutes later. 'So they were together,' Lucy
said to herself. 'Exciting news! Well, not for me.'

She did not want to think about it. On the bus home
she looked out of the window, but everywhere she saw
hearts and red roses.

Everywhere Lucy saw hearts and red roses.

'Forget Valentine's Day!' Lucy said to herself when she got home. 'I'm going to watch a film.' But when she opened her door, there was a piece of paper on the floor. The message on the paper said, 'Watch the local news on TV at 18:00.' There was no name.

'Who wrote this?' Lucy said. 'Watch the news? Why?'

She turned on the TV and went to make a cup of coffee. Suddenly she heard the name 'Sam Morris' and she ran back to the TV.

'It's Valentine's Day,' said the TV reporter, 'and Sam put a message in the Sunflower Café for his girlfriend Lucy. Sam made all the cakes, and he put them in the window last night. You can see them here.'

Lucy looked. There in the window of the Sunflower Café was a big red heart cake. Around it were lots of little cakes, and they made a message – a special message for Lucy.

'There's the message, but where's Lucy?' the reporter said. 'She often comes to the Sunflower Café, but she didn't come today. And she isn't answering her phone. Is Sam going to have a happy Valentine's Day? What's your answer, Lucy?'

But Lucy didn't tell him. She didn't even stop to turn off the TV. She got her coat and ran out of the door. She had a very important message for Sam. She didn't want to phone him, she didn't want to send a text. She wanted to give him the message, face to face.

A message for Lucy . . .

Friday, 15th February, evening

The next evening, Becky arrived at Lucy's house. Sam opened the door.

'Congratulations, Sam!' said Becky. 'And Lucy too.'

'Oh, thank you, Becky. Come on in,' Lucy said.

'Congratulations, Sam! And Lucy, too,' said Becky.

'I've got some champagne for you,' Becky said. 'Here.'

Sam took the bottle. 'Wonderful!' he said. 'Let's drink it now.' He went away to open the bottle. Becky turned to Lucy.

'You look so happy!' she said. 'But what happened yesterday? I was really worried, you know. You didn't tell me anything on the phone this morning.'

Lucy laughed, but her face was red. 'I know. I'm sorry,' she said.

'But why didn't you answer my phone messages or my texts?' said Becky. 'Come on! Tell me everything!'

'Well,' Lucy said, 'I went to the café on the 13th, and I was at the door and . . . and I saw you inside with Sam. You looked so happy together. Then you kissed Sam, and he kissed you. And on Monday, you remember, you talked about a 'surprise'. Well, I thought that was the surprise – you and Sam.'

'Oh Lucy!' said Becky. 'That wasn't the surprise! Sam and I talked about Valentine's Day. He wanted to make a special Valentine's Day for you. So I said to him, "What do you do best, Sam? You make wonderful cakes. So make her a cake!" And he thought about it, and he had a better idea – he made lots of cakes. I kissed him because I was so excited for you.'

'Well,' said Lucy, 'when I saw you two, I got the wrong idea. And I went home. I didn't want to talk to anyone. And I really didn't want to talk to *you* – or Sam!'

Becky laughed. 'Oh Lucy,' she said. 'You thought – me and Sam . . . Well, it doesn't matter now. And I wanted to tell you – on Tuesday night at Marco's Club I met this man. He's called Matt, and he's really nice. But go on with your story.'

'On Valentine's Day I didn't answer my phone, and Sam couldn't leave the café,' Lucy said. 'So his friend Nick put a message under my door. It said, "Watch the local news on TV at 18:00." And at last I saw the cakes, and the message – and I *ran* to the Sunflower Café.'

'And now it's all OK,' said Becky. 'Can I see your ring? Oh, that's beautiful.'

Sam brought three glasses of champagne.

'To Lucy and Sam!' said Becky, and they all drank.

Sam looked at his watch, and turned on the TV. 'Hey, Becky, watch this,' he said. 'This is the end of the story.' After a few minutes the local news began, and they saw the same reporter from the day before. He was outside the window of the Sunflower Café.

'Everyone wanted to know the answer to Sam's question to Lucy yesterday,' the reporter said. 'Well, Sam got his answer. Lucy came to the Sunflower Café last night after she saw the news on TV. And this was her answer – here in the window!'

The television camera went closer to the window. In the window there were just four cakes now. There was the big red heart cake, and three little cakes above it.

'Lucy wanted to do that. She took my little cakes and wrote her answer with them,' said Sam. He gave Lucy a little kiss.

Becky laughed. 'Oh, you two!' she said. 'You're – wonderful!'

The Bridge

∘ ◆ ∘

Alma closed the door of her parents' home, and she and her friend Barbara stood in the sun for a moment.

'Your mother is so nice, Alma,' said Barbara. 'She said to me, "We love to see Alma's friends." She wants me to stay for a week!'

Alma smiled. 'She likes you, Barbara. You're a good friend to me, and my mother knows that,' she said. She looked around her at the street. 'After six years away, this city feels very different to me.'

Barbara smiled. 'Yes,' she said, 'after your six years in Vienna, you're more Austrian than I am. But everything feels different now, it's true. Six long years of study — and now we're doctors!'

'And next month everything changes for you again,' Alma said. 'A new life in Salzburg. I'm really happy for you.'

'A new life, a new city, a new hospital,' said Barbara. 'It's a famous hospital, too. I'm lucky to get work there.' She turned to her friend. 'But what about you, Alma? What are you going to do? Are you going back to live in Vienna again? Or are you going to look for work here?'

'I don't know,' said Alma slowly. 'Before I can answer

that question, I need to tell you a story. The story of Nina.' They started walking to the river, and Alma began her story.

'I need to tell you a story,' said Alma. 'The story of Nina . . .'

Nina was my little sister. She was beautiful – much more beautiful than me, with her black hair and green eyes. And she was full of life, and clever too.

There were always boyfriends at the door, but they changed all the time. Then when she was eighteen, she began to study at the university. One day she came home with a smile on her face.

'What is it, Nina?' I asked. 'You look excited about something. Or is it somebody? Tell me!'

'I met someone today,' she said happily. 'He's called Dragan and he's studying maths too. And he's . . . he's *wonderful!*'

'That's great, Nina,' I said. 'Where in the city does he live?'

My sister did not answer this question. She began to talk about a party on Friday night. I looked at her face carefully. I knew my little sister very well.

'Nina,' I said. 'Come on, tell me. Where does Dragan live?'

Again, Nina said nothing, but I knew the answer. It was bad news – bad news for Nina, bad news for our parents, bad news for everyone.

Two weeks later, Nina brought Dragan to our house. Dragan was tall and dark, with bright eyes and a quick smile. He loved Nina, and she loved him – we could all see that. Dragan had dinner with us, and then we had coffee and talked. Then my father spoke.

'Dragan,' he said, 'your people are not our people.'

I looked at Nina. She was quiet, and watched my father carefully, but she said nothing. Dragan looked worried.

'We live on this side of the river, and your people live on the other side,' my father said. 'We have our places of worship, and you have yours. We are different. We have our ways, and your people have their ways. It was like that when I was a boy, and it is still like that now.'

Then he smiled.

Dragan loved Nina, and she loved him – we could all see that.

'But we can be friends,' he said. 'You are a good man, and my daughter loves you. Anybody can see that. Our door is always open to you, Dragan.'

'Thank you,' said Dragan quietly. And Nina smiled – at him, at my father, at me, at everybody.

After that, they were always together. At the university, at home, in town – it was always Nina and Dragan. They studied together and went to parties together. They were two young people, happy and in love.

And then the war began. At first things were difficult, but they could still meet sometimes. But then things began to change. When the university closed, Nina and Dragan could not see each other every day. They talked on the phone, but it was not the same.

'I can't live without him,' Nina said.

'I can't live without him,' Nina said to us one night, with tears on her face. 'I must see him! I must.'

'Nina, you can't cross the bridge,' my father said. 'It's dangerous for you over there. There are men with guns everywhere, and they watch the bridge night and day. And Dragan can't come here – not now. We must all wait. Perhaps one day you can see him again.'

'Wait?' said Nina, and the tears came to her eyes again. 'For how long?'

A week later, Nina left our house very early one morning. Nobody heard her. Dragan left his house, too, and they both walked carefully and quietly to the bridge. They just wanted to see each other. Nina left a message for us in her room.

'I'm not going onto the bridge,' the message said, 'but I must see him. I can't wait any longer.'

We waited all day. Where was she? My mother phoned all our friends, but nobody had any news. Then that evening an old friend of the family came to the door.

'I have some terrible news,' he said. 'I'm so sorry, so sorry.'

At once my mother began to cry. My father put his arm around her. 'Tell us,' he said. 'It's about my daughter, yes? My little Nina . . .'

'It happened this morning,' our friend said. 'On the bridge. Your daughter saw her boyfriend Dragan on the other side. She called his name, and he ran onto the

'*Your daughter ran onto the bridge at once.*'

bridge – and somebody shot him. When he fell, she ran onto the bridge at once. She took him in her arms, but somebody shot her too. They died on the bridge together. We are trying to bring their bodies back, but it's very difficult. I am very sorry.'

I went to Nina's room. Next to her bed, there was a photo of her and Dragan. She told me once, 'I can't live without him.' And it was true. But now they are together – for ever.

So we waited. Those were terrible days. Nobody said very much, and my mother cried a lot. In my room at night, I cried too. And then, on a beautiful spring day, we went to a hill above the town. It was sunny all day. Nina loved the sun, I remembered. And there we buried them together – my sister Nina, and her Dragan.

❦

For a few minutes, the two women did not speak. They walked slowly along by the river. The water was bright in the sunlight.

Then Barbara said, 'And when did you leave and go to Austria?'

'A week later,' Alma said. 'My parents sent me to my mother's sister Ana in Vienna. I did not want to leave them, but it was dangerous here – more dangerous every day. They did not want to lose two daughters. Ana was good to me – she understood. She helped me to begin my studies again.'

'And now you are back in your home town,' said Barbara. 'Why now?'

'When the war ended,' Alma said, 'I wanted to come back. But I wasn't ready. "Finish your studies first," my parents said, and they were right. But now it's the right time. I needed to see my family, and I needed to go to the bridge.'

Alma stopped, and turned to her friend. Her face was white. 'And there it is,' she said, very quietly. 'Just along the river. Look. You can see it now.'

'And there it is,' Alma said. 'Just along the river.'

Barbara took her friend's arm. 'Let's go over there to that café,' she said. 'You need to sit down.'

'The Bridge Café,' said Alma. 'I remember it – Nina often waited for Dragan there. Yes, let's go there – I feel close to Nina there.'

They crossed the road and sat down at a table outside the café. They both had coffee, and Alma began to look better.

'Are you OK?' asked Barbara.

'Yes, thanks,' said Alma. 'I just need some time – and some more coffee perhaps.'

Barbara felt the warm sun on her face. 'This is a difficult day for Alma,' she thought. 'But the sun's shining, and people are doing the usual things – working, driving around, shopping, talking, having coffee . . . Perhaps that can help her.'

Alma and Barbara had another coffee, and watched the river. Just then a big black car stopped near the bridge. A beautiful young woman in a long white dress got out of the car with a young man. She carried a bouquet of white flowers in one hand, and the young man held her other hand. They walked onto the bridge, and when they got to the middle, they stopped. The young woman took two flowers from her bouquet. She dropped one flower into the river, and her husband dropped the second flower.

Alma and Barbara watched all this. 'What are they

'*Love is more important than war.*'

doing?' Alma whispered. 'Find out for me, Barbara. Ask somebody.'

Barbara turned to a man at the next table. 'Excuse me,' she said. 'I'm a visitor here. Can you answer a question for me?'

'Yes, of course,' the man said. 'What do you want to know?'

'Those two young people on the bridge,' said Barbara. 'What are they doing? Why are they dropping flowers into the water?'

'It's their wedding day,' said the man. 'In the war, two young lovers died on the bridge. They were called Nina and Dragan. We don't want to forget them. Now, after a wedding, people come here and drop two flowers into the river – one for Nina, one for Dragan. Watch them now – they are saying their names.'

Barbara was afraid to look at Alma's face. Alma sat so still, so still.

On the bridge, the man and woman watched the flowers in the water for a moment. The man put his arm around his young wife. Then they walked slowly back to the car and drove away.

'Who did it first? I don't know,' said the man at the next table. 'But now everybody comes here on their wedding day. We all remember the war, of course we do, but we must remember love too. Love is more important than war.'

'Thank you,' said Barbara. 'Thank you very much for telling us that story.'

She looked at Alma's white face. 'Come,' she said quietly. 'Let's walk onto the bridge together.'

She took Alma's arm and they walked onto the bridge. At the middle of the bridge Barbara stopped, and looked out over the river.

'Look,' she said to Alma. 'The flowers are still there. Do you see? Flowers for Nina and Dragan. That's so beautiful.'

The two white flowers were bright in the sun.

'Love is more important than war,' Alma whispered. There were tears on her face, and she watched the flowers for a long time. Then she looked at Barbara, and slowly smiled.

'Barbara, I know the answer to my question,' she said. 'I can live here again. This is my home.'

They walked off the bridge. The two flowers, together in the water, moved slowly away on the river.

GLOSSARY

bike another word for bicycle

blonde a very light yellow colour (e.g. blonde hair)

bouquet an attractive group of flowers, often given as a present

boyfriend a boy or man who a girl is in love with

bury to put a dead person in the ground

café a place where people can buy a drink and something to eat

cake a sweet food made from flour, eggs, sugar, and butter and cooked in the oven

canteen a place at school or work where people can buy meals

champagne a French white wine with a lot of bubbles

cheek the soft part of your face below your eye

clap to hit your hands together to show that you like something

clinic a place where you can go to get special help from a doctor

club a place where people go to dance, listen to music, etc.

congratulations you say this to somebody when you are pleased about something they have done

cool! (*informal*) very good, great, interesting, wonderful, different

Facebook a social networking website where people can send messages, photos, etc. to their friends

fall (*past tense* **fell**) to go down quickly from a high place

festival a few days when many bands play music, in one place

glasses pieces of glass over the eyes to help you to see better

great (*informal*) very good, very nice, wonderful

hang out with (*informal*) to spend time with

heart the place inside you where your feelings are; also, a shape like this ♥, used to mean 'love'

idea a plan or thought in your head

kiss to touch someone with the lips to show love

list a lot of names, questions, etc. written down one after another

local   belonging to the place where you live
lucky   having good luck (when nice things happen by chance)
maths   the study of numbers, measurements, and shapes
message   words that one person sends to another
mobile phone   a phone that you can carry around with you
music   sounds that are nice or exciting to listen to
parents   your mother and father
physiotherapy   the use of exercises to help muscles and joints
poor   a word that you use when you feel sorry for someone
race   a competition to see who can run, drive, etc. the fastest
really   very much; in fact
reporter   a person who reads the news on radio, television, etc.
ring   a circle of metal that you wear on your finger
salsa dancing   a kind of fast, exciting Latin American dancing
seat   a place where you can sit
shine   to send out light; to be bright
shoot (*past tense* **shot**)   to hurt or kill a person with a gun
shout   to speak or call out very loudly
social committee   a group of people who plan fun things for
   other people to do together
study   to spend time learning about something
surprise (*n*)   something that you did not know and did not
   expect
surprised   when you feel or show surprise
tear (*n*)   water that comes from your eyes when you cry
tent   a kind of small house made of cloth
terrible   something terrible makes you very afraid or unhappy
text message   a short written message sent on a mobile phone
towel   a piece of cloth that you use to dry your body
university   a place where people study after they leave school
wedding   the day when a man and woman marry
worried   unhappy, afraid that something bad is going to happen
worship (**places of**)   buildings where people talk to their God

The Bridge
and Other Love Stories

ACTIVITIES

ACTIVITIES

Before Reading

1 **Read the introduction on the first page of the book, and the back cover. What do you know now about the stories? Tick one box for each sentence.**

		YES	NO
1	Luke and Gemma make a plan for a holiday.	☐	☒
2	Sam has something exciting for Lucy.	☒	☐
3	There is a surprise for Becky at the Sunflower Café.	☐	☒
4	Luke is good at talking to girls.	☐	☒
5	Alma left her home town six years ago.	☒	☐
6	Alma forgot about Nina when she left her home town.	☐	☒

2 **What happens in these stories? Can you guess? Choose one answer for each question.**

1 In *Plan for Love*, Luke has a lot of questions for . . .
   a) himself.
   b) a beautiful girl at work.
   c) Gemma.
   d) his family.

2 In *The Maker of Cakes*, Lucy's friend Becky . . .
   a) takes Lucy's boyfriend.
   b) gets a job in the Sunflower Café.
   c) helps Lucy's boyfriend.
   d) buys a cake for Lucy.

3 At the end of *The Maker of Cakes,* Lucy is going to . . .

a) marry Sam.

b) leave Sam.

c) work with Sam.

d) go on the TV news.

4 In *The Bridge* Alma learns something new about . . .

a) her family.

b) her friend Barbara.

c) her sister Nina.

d) the people of her home town.

3 Six of the words in the chart are in all three stories, and there are also two more words from each story. Can you guess which words are in which stories? Put ticks in the chart.

	ALL stories	Plan for Love	The Maker of Cakes	The Bridge
bike				X
coffee	X			
friend	X			
gun		X		
happy	X			
love	X			
music	X			
question		X		
ring			X	
river				X
roses			X	
smile	X			

ACTIVITIES

After Reading

1 **Match these parts of sentences. First choose the right name for the first part, then choose the right pronoun** *(he / she / they)* **for the second part.**

Alma, Barbara, Becky, Charlotte, Dragan, Gemma, Lucy, Luke, Nina, Sam

1 _____ loved Nina very much, . . .

2 _____ wanted to talk to Charlotte, . . .

3 _____ saw Dragan across the bridge, . . .

4 _____ saw Sam's cakes on the TV news, . . .

5 _____ was in love with Luke, . . .

6 _____ was excited about Sam's idea, . . .

7 _____ was afraid to go back to her home town . . .

8 _____ wanted to go to Eastwater . . .

9 _____ made some cakes for Lucy, . . .

10 _____ met her friend Alma . . .

11 so *he / she* ran to the café.

12 when *she / they* studied medicine together in Vienna.

13 but *he / she* was just a friend to her.

14 because *he / she* loved shopping.

15 and *he / she* loved him too.

16 but *he / she* couldn't find the right words.

17 so *he / she* kissed him in the café.

18 and *he / she* put them in the window.

19 because *he / she* could not forget the sad story of her
     sister Nina.

20 and *he / she* called his name.

2 **Some months after Barbara's visit, Alma wrote to her in
   Salzburg. Use these words to complete her letter (one word
   for each gap).**

*about, boyfriend, children's, drop, flowers, hospital, into,
life, love, news, nice, river, tired, usually, visit*

> *Dear Barbara*
>
> *How are you? How is _____ in Salzburg? Are
> you very busy? I've got a job at the _____ here, and
> I'm working hard. I'm working in the _____ clinic,
> and I love it. But I get very _____!*
>
> *I often walk along by the _____, and I remember
> our first _____ to the bridge. Some days there are
> a lot of _____ in the water. I _____ to see them
> there. Sometimes I cry, but _____ I smile, and I
> think _____ Nina. And I've got some _____ for
> you. I've got a new _____ – he's a doctor too, and
> his name is Mario. He's really very _____. Perhaps
> one day I can _____ a flower _____ the river for
> Nina!*
>
> *With love*
> *Alma*

3 Here is a new illustration for one of the stories. Find the best place to put the picture, and answer these questions.

The picture goes on page _____, in the story _____.

1 Who is the girl, and where is she running to?
2 Why is she going there?
3 What is she going to do when she gets there?

Now write a caption for the illustration.

Caption: _____

4 Use the clues below to complete this crossword with words from the story.

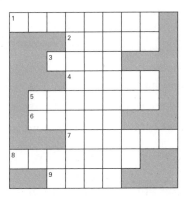

1 A few days when many bands play music, in one place.

2 These fall from your eyes when you cry.

3 This means 'great!' or 'wonderful!'

4 The part of your face at the side below your eye.

5 Your mother and father are your _____.

6 To speak very loudly.

7 You walk on this to get across a river.

8 The day when two people get married.

9 Another word for 'bicycle'.

5 Now look at the completed crossword and find the hidden nine-letter word in it. Complete these sentences.

1 The hidden word is _____.

2 This word comes from the story _____.

6 **Sam and Becky talked about Sam's new idea for the cakes. Put their conversation in the right order, and write in the speakers' names. Sam speaks first (number 2).**

1 _____ 'And they have a message – come and see.'

2 _____ 'You remember your idea about a cake for Lucy.'

3 _____ 'Well, I had a better idea. I made lots of cakes.'

4 _____ 'Of course! Lucy is going to love this.'

5 _____ 'Lots of cakes! That's a great idea.'

6 _____ 'Oh Sam, tomorrow is going to be so exciting. I can't wait!'

7 _____ 'Do you think so? Do you think she'll like it?'

8 _____ 'Yes – did you do it, Sam? What's it like?'

9 _____ 'Oh, each little cake has a letter . . . "Please marry me Lucy." That's so cool, Sam!'

10_____ 'Well, I'm going to put them in the window later this evening – and then tomorrow . . .'

7 **Gemma is thinking about Luke while she makes some questions for him. Use these words to complete the passage (one word for each gap).**

answer, bike, can, got, interested, interesting, kind, loves, music, must, never, questions, too, understand

I really don't _____, Luke – why are you _____ in Charlotte? She's not your _____ of girl! Can't you see that? But I _____ think of some_____. OK. Let's start with _____. *Do you like the Tree Rats?* Huh, I _____ answer that one for Charlotte – and the _____ is No! I know – *What kind of music do you*

like? That's good. Now – swimming. Luke _____ swimming.
Me _____. And Charlotte? She _____ goes swimming, I
think. Oh – and Charlotte on a _____! That's an _____ idea!
So, next question is – *Have you _____ a bike?*

8 **Do you agree or disagree with these ideas? Explain why.**

1 It is important for a boyfriend or girlfriend to like doing
the same things as you.
2 Love is more important than war.
3 It is better to love and die young than to live a long time
without love.
4 When you are in love, it is easy to get the wrong idea
about people.

9 **How did you feel about the people in these stories? Choose
a name for the first gaps, and then complete the sentences in
your own words. Use as many words as you like.**

*Charlotte / Gemma / Luke / Lucy / Becky / Sam / Alma /
Barbara / Dragan / Nina*

1 I felt sorry for _____ because _____.
2 I did not feel sorry for _____ because _____.
3 I felt pleased for _____ because _____.
4 I felt happy for _____ when _____.
5 I liked _____ because _____.
6 I did not like _____ because _____.

ABOUT THE AUTHOR

Christine Lindop was born in New Zealand and taught English in France and Spain before settling in Great Britain. She is the Series Editor for Bookworms Factfiles, and has written or co-written more than twenty books, including several Bookworms titles – *Sally's Phone, Red Roses,* and *The Girl with Red Hair* (Human Interest, Starter), *Ned Kelly: A True Story* (True Stories, Stage 1), *Weddings* (Factfiles, Stage 1) and *Australia and New Zealand* (Factfiles, Stage 3). She has also adapted three volumes of short stories for Bookworms World Stories: *The Long White Cloud: Stories from New Zealand* (Stage 3), *Doors to a Wider Place: Stories from Australia* (Stage 4), and *The Price of Peace: Stories from Africa* (Stage 4). She has written for the Oxford Dominoes and Dolphin Readers series, and has worked on many other Oxford graded readers series, including Classic Tales, Hotshot Puzzles, and Storylines.

The idea for the story called *The Bridge* came from a true story. The reporter Kurt Schork wrote about two young lovers, Bosko Brckic and Admira Ismic, who died in Sarajevo in the Bosnian war in 1993 (you can read his story at http://www. ksmemorial.com). 'This is *not* their story,' says Christine, 'though some of the things about it are the same. But their story made me think about love, and war, and the very old idea of lovers who are divided by war. I wanted to write a story that had love, and sadness, but hope as well. Nina and Dragan are not forgotten, and Alma has a happy future in front of her.'

OXFORD BOOKWORMS LIBRARY

Classics • Crime & Mystery • Factfiles • Fantasy & Horror
Human Interest • Playscripts • Thriller & Adventure
True Stories • World Stories

The OXFORD BOOKWORMS LIBRARY provides enjoyable reading in English, with a wide range of classic and modern fiction, non-fiction, and plays. It includes original and adapted texts in seven carefully graded language stages, which take learners from beginner to advanced level. An overview is given on the next pages.

All Stage 1 titles are available as audio recordings, as well as over eighty other titles from Starter to Stage 6. All Starters and many titles at Stages 1 to 4 are specially recommended for younger learners. Every Bookworm is illustrated, and Starters and Factfiles have full-colour illustrations.

The OXFORD BOOKWORMS LIBRARY also offers extensive support. Each book contains an introduction to the story, notes about the author, a glossary, and activities. Additional resources include tests and worksheets, and answers for these and for the activities in the books. There is advice on running a class library, using audio recordings, and the many ways of using Oxford Bookworms in reading programmes. Resource materials are available on the website <www.oup.com/bookworms>.

The *Oxford Bookworms Collection* is a series for advanced learners. It consists of volumes of short stories by well-known authors, both classic and modern. Texts are not abridged or adapted in any way, but carefully selected to be accessible to the advanced student.

You can find details and a full list of titles in the *Oxford Bookworms Library Catalogue* and *Oxford English Language Teaching Catalogues*, and on the website <www.oup.com/bookworms>.

THE OXFORD BOOKWORMS LIBRARY
GRADING AND SAMPLE EXTRACTS

STARTER • 250 HEADWORDS

present simple – present continuous – imperative –
can/cannot, must – *going to* (future) – simple gerunds ...

Her phone is ringing – but where is it?

Sally gets out of bed and looks in her bag. No phone. She looks under the bed. No phone. Then she looks behind the door. There is her phone. Sally picks up her phone and answers it. *Sally's Phone*

STAGE 1 • 400 HEADWORDS

... past simple – coordination with *and, but, or* –
subordination with *before, after, when, because, so* ...

I knew him in Persia. He was a famous builder and I worked with him there. For a time I was his friend, but not for long. When he came to Paris, I came after him – I wanted to watch him. He was a very clever, very dangerous man. *The Phantom of the Opera*

STAGE 2 • 700 HEADWORDS

... present perfect – *will* (future) – (*don't*) *have to, must not, could* –
comparison of adjectives – simple *if* clauses – past continuous –
tag questions – *ask/tell* + infinitive ...

While I was writing these words in my diary, I decided what to do. I must try to escape. I shall try to get down the wall outside. The window is high above the ground, but I have to try. I shall take some of the gold with me – if I escape, perhaps it will be helpful later. *Dracula*

STAGE 3 • 1000 HEADWORDS

... should, may – present perfect continuous – *used to* – past perfect –
causative – relative clauses – indirect statements ...

Of course, it was most important that no one should see
Colin, Mary, or Dickon entering the secret garden. So Colin
gave orders to the gardeners that they must all keep away
from that part of the garden in future. *The Secret Garden*

STAGE 4 • 1400 HEADWORDS

*... past perfect continuous – passive (simple forms) –
would* conditional clauses – indirect questions –
relatives with *where/when* – gerunds after prepositions/phrases ...

I was glad. Now Hyde could not show his face to the world
again. If he did, every honest man in London would be proud
to report him to the police. *Dr Jekyll and Mr Hyde*

STAGE 5 • 1800 HEADWORDS

... future continuous – future perfect –
passive (modals, continuous forms) –
would have conditional clauses – modals + perfect infinitive ...

If he had spoken Estella's name, I would have hit him. I was so
angry with him, and so depressed about my future, that I could
not eat the breakfast. Instead I went straight to the old house.
Great Expectations

STAGE 6 • 2500 HEADWORDS

... passive (infinitives, gerunds) – advanced modal meanings –
clauses of concession, condition

When I stepped up to the piano, I was confident. It was as if I
knew that the prodigy side of me really did exist. And when I
started to play, I was so caught up in how lovely I looked that
I didn't worry how I would sound. *The Joy Luck Club*

BOOKWORMS · TRUE STORIES · STAGE 1

Ned Kelly: A True Story

CHRISTINE LINDOP

When he was a boy, he was poor and hungry. When he was a young man, he was still poor and hungry. He learnt how to steal horses, he learnt how to fight, he learnt how to live – outside the law. Australia in the 1870s was a hard, wild place. Rich people had land, poor people didn't. So the rich got richer, and the poor stayed poor.

Some say Ned Kelly was a bad man. Some say he was a good man but the law was bad. This is the true story of Australia's most famous outlaw.

BOOKWORMS · HUMAN INTEREST · STAGE 1

Little Lord Fauntleroy

FRANCES HODGSON BURNETT

Retold by Jennifer Bassett

Cedric Errol is seven years old. He lives with his mother in a little house in New York. They don't have much money, but mother and son are very good friends. Cedric is a kind, friendly little boy, and everybody likes him. His father was English, but he is now dead, and Cedric and his mother are alone in the world.

But one day a lawyer arrives from England with some very surprising news about Cedric's grandfather . . .